To:

From:

Date:

Hear My Prayer

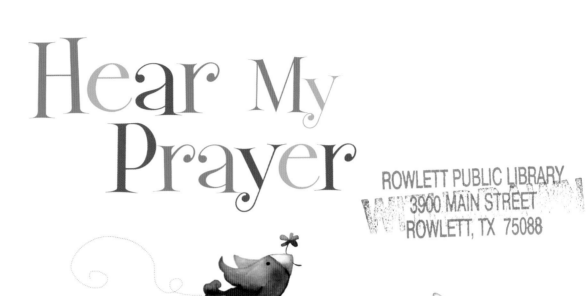

By
Lee Bennett Hopkins

Illustrated by
Gretchen "Gigi" Moore

ZONDERkidz

ZONDERVAN.com/
AUTHORTRACKER
follow your favorite authors

"Call to me and I will answer you . . ."

—Jeremiah 33:3

To my goddaughter,

Alexis Maria Garcia,

& her brother, Jack Eugene

LBH

ZONDERKIDZ

Hear My Prayer
Copyright © 2011 by Lee Bennett Hopkins
Illustrations © 2011 by Gretchen "Gigi" Moore

Acknowledgements:
Thanks are due to Curtis Brown, Ltd. for use of "Prayer at Suppertime" by Rebecca
Kai Dotlich. Copyright © 2010 by Rebecca Kai Dotlich; "Good Night" and "Your
Touch" by Lee Bennett Hopkins. Copyright © 2010 by Lee Bennett Hopkins. Used by
permission of Curtis Brown, Ltd.

Requests for information should be addressed to:

Zonderkidz, Grand Rapids, Michigan 49530

Library of Congress Cataloging-in-Publication Data

Hear my prayer / [selected] by Lee Bennett Hopkins.
    p. cm.
  ISBN 978-0-310-71811-6 (hardcover)
  1. Prayers—Juvenile literature. I. Hopkins, Lee Bennett.
  BV265.H38 2009
  242'.82—dc22   2009007188

Editor: Mary Hassinger
Art direction: Jody Langley
Design: Sarah Molegraaf

Printed in China

Hear My Prayer

Selections by Lee Bennett Hopkins

Table of Contents

Prayer

Now, before I run to play
Let me not forget to pray
To God who kept me through the night
And woke me with the morning light.

Help me, Lord, to love you more
Than I have ever loved before,
In my work and in my play,
Please be with me through each day.

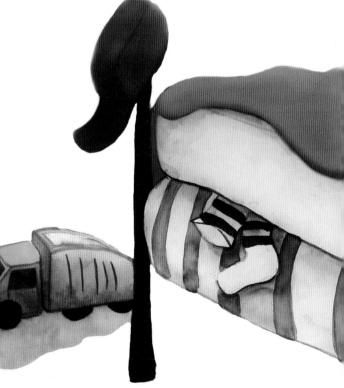

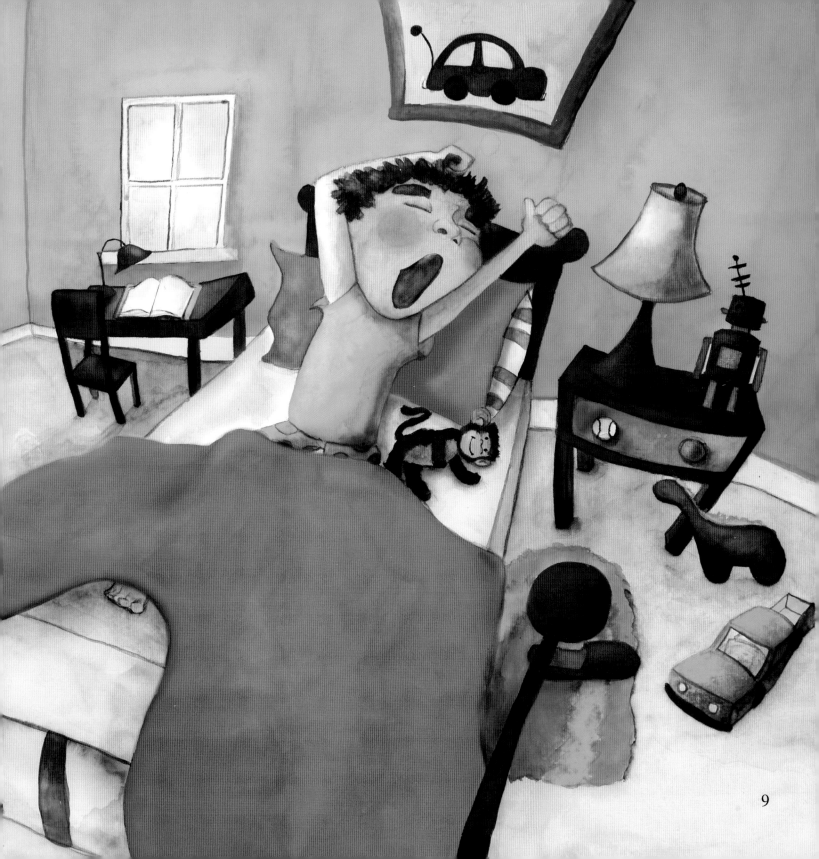

Busy

Dear God:

You know how busy
I must be today,

If I forget you,
Please
Do not forget me.

Friends

Dear God:

Thank you for my friend next door,
For my friend across the street,

Please help me to be a friend
To each and every one I meet.

Blessings

God made the world
So broad, so grand,
Filled with blessing
From his hand.

He made the sky
So high, so blue,
And all us little children, too.

Earth

The earth has a carpet
All shining fresh and green.

It's made of little blades of grass
With flowers in between.

And on this carpet
Happy and free,

We dance our thanks,
Dear Lord, to Thee.

Your Touch

Dear Lord,

You touch us all —
Doctors, nurses,
Firefighters,
Teachers, crossing guards,
Window washers, writers.

Yet always remember
To give your touch
To Grandma and Grandpa
Who I love so much.

Lee Bennett Hopkins

Parents

Dear Lord,
Keep my parents in your love.

Lord,
Bless them and keep them.

Lord,
Keep them for many more years
So I can take care of them.

Peace

Dear Lord,
Creator of the world,
Help us love one another,
Help us care for one another,
As sister or as brother.

May friendship grow
From nation to nation.

Bring peace to our world
Dear Lord of Creation.

Prayer at Suppertime

Bless this bread we share.
Bless our voices as we pray.

Bless this food.

Bring us goodness
     As you do, Lord,
      Each and every day.

Rebecca Kai Dotlich

All Those That I Love

God bless all those that I love.
God bless all those that love me.

God bless all those
That love those that I love.

And all those that love those
That love me.

25

from
Pippa Passes

The lark's on the wing;
The snail's on the thorn:

God's in His Heaven—
All's right with the world.

Robert Browning

And God Bless Me

I see the moon.
The moon sees me.

God bless the moon,
And God bless me.

Good Night

Dear God:

Day is done.
Play is played.

Friends are near.
We're safe from fear.

Thank you
For the moon afar,

Thank you, God,
For who you are.

Lee Bennett Hopkins